D1119334

Borders & Frames

Memories of a Lifetime

Sterling Publishing Co., Inc. New York

A Sterling/Chapelle Book

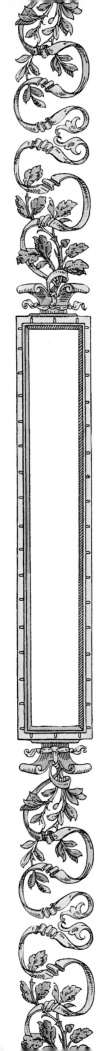

Contributing designer: Paige Hill

If you have any questions or comments, please contact:
 Chapelle, Ltd., Inc., P.O. Box 9252, Ogden, UT 84409
 (801) 621-2777 • (801) 621-2788 Fax
 e-mail: chapelle@chapelleltd.com
 Web site: www.chapelleltd.com

The designs and illustrations in this book may be used for personal graphic, craft, and publication applications without special permission and free of charge. Commercial use of artwork contained in this volume is forbidden under law without the written permission of the publisher.

10 9 8 7 6 5 4 3

Published by Sterling Publishing Co., Inc.
387 Park Avenue South, New York, NY 10016
© 2005 by Sterling Publishing Co., Inc.
Distributed in Canada by Sterling Publishing
c/o Canadian Manda Group, 165 Dufferin Street
Toronto, Ontario, Canada M6K 3H6
Distributed in Great Britain by Chrysalis Books Group PLC,
The Chrysalis Building, Bramley Road, London W10 6SP, England
Distributed in Australia by Capricorn Link (Australia) Pty. Ltd.
P. O. Box 704, Windsor, NSW 2756, Australia
Printed and Bound in China
All Rights Reserved

Sterling ISBN 1-4027-1997-3

Introduction

Imagine having hundreds of rare, vintage images right at your fingertips. With our *Memories of a Lifetime* series, that's exactly what you get. We've scoured antique stores, estate sales, and other outlets to find one-of-a-kind images to give your projects the flair that only old-time artwork can provide. From Victorian postcards to hand-painted beautiful borders and frames, it would take years to acquire a collection like this. However, with this easy-to-use resource, you'll have them all—right here, right now.

Each image has been reproduced to the highest quality standard for photocopying and scanning; reduce or enlarge them to suit your needs. A CD-Rom containing all of the images in digital form is included, enabling you to use them for any computer project over and again. If you prefer to use them as they're printed, simply cut them out—they're printed on one side only.

Perfect for paper crafting, scrapbooking, and fabric transfers, *Memories of a Lifetime* books will inspire you to explore new avenues of creativity. We've included a sampling of ideas to get you started, but the best part is using your imagination to create your own fabulous projects. Be sure to look for other books in this series as we continue to search the markets for wonderful vintage images.

How to Use this Book

General Instructions:

These images are printed on one side only, making it easy to simply cut out the desired image. However, you'll probably want to use them again, so we have included a CD-Rom which contains all of the images individually as well as in the page layout form. The CDs can be used with both PC and Mac formats. Just pop in the disk. On a PC, the file will immediately open to the Home page, which will walk you through how to view and print the images. For Macintosh® users, you will simply double-click on the icon to open. The images may also be incorporated into your computer projects using simple imaging software that you can purchase specifically for this purpose—a perfect choice for digital scrapbooking. The reference numbers printed on the back of each image in the book are the same ones used on the CD, which will allow you to easily find the image you are looking for. The numbering consists of the book abbreviation, the page number, the image number, and the file format. The first file number (located next to the page number) is for the entire page. For example, BF01-001.jpg would be the entire image for page 1 of *Borders & Frames*. The second file number is for the top-right image. The numbers continue in a counterclockwise fashion.

Once you have resized your images, added text, created a scrapbook page, etc., you are ready to print them out. Printing on cream or white cardstock, particularly a textured variety, creates a more authentic look. You won't be able to tell that it's a reproduction! If you don't have access to a computer or printer, that's ok. Most photocopy centers can resize and print your images for a nominal fee, or they have do-it-yourself machines that are easy to use.

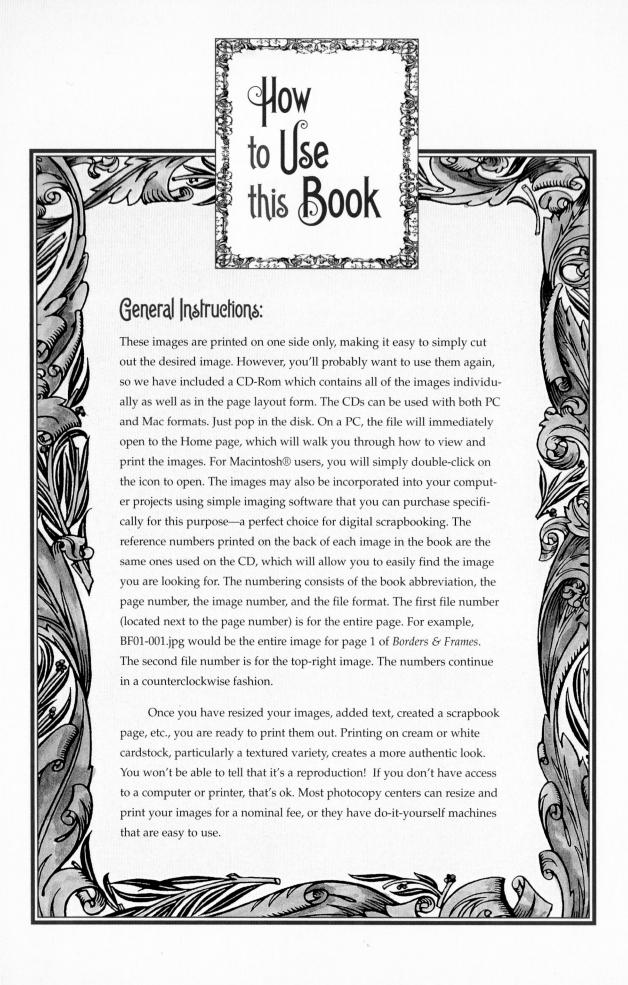

Ideas for using the images:

Scrapbooking: These images are perfect for both heritage and modern scrapbook pages. Simply use the image as a frame, accent piece, or border. For those of you with limited time, or limited design ability, the page layouts in this book have been created so that you can use them as they are. Simply print out or photocopy the desired page, attach a photograph into one of the boxes, and you have a beautiful scrapbook page in minutes. For a little dimension, add a ribbon or charm. Be sure to print your images onto acid-free cardstock so the pages will last a lifetime.

Cards: Some computer programs allow images to be inserted into a card template, simplifying cardmaking. If this is not an option, simply use the images as accent pieces on the front or inside of the card. Use a bone folder to score the card's fold to create a more professional look.

Decoupage/Collage Projects: For decoupage or collage projects, photocopy or print the image onto a thinner paper such as copier paper. Thin paper adheres to projects more effectively. Decoupage medium glues and seals the project, creating a gloss or matte finish when dry, thus protecting the image. Vintage images are beautiful when decoupaged to cigar boxes, glass plates, and even wooden plaques. The possibilities are endless.

Fabric Arts: Vintage images can be used in just about any fabric craft imaginable: wall hangings, quilts, bags, or baby bibs. Either transfer the image onto the fabric by using a special iron-on paper, or by printing the image directly onto the fabric, using a temporary iron-on stabilizer that stabilizes the fabric to feed through a printer. These items are available at most craft and sewing stores. If the item will be washed, it is better to print directly on the fabric. For either method, follow the instructions on the package.

Wood Transfers: It is now possible to "print" images on wood. Use this exciting technique to create vintage plaques, clocks, frames, and more. A simple, inexpensive transfer tool is available at most large craft or home improvement stores, or online from various manufacturers. You simply place the photocopy of the image you want, face down, onto the surface and use the tool to transfer the image onto the wood. This process requires a copy from a laser printer, which means you will probably have to get your copies made at a copy center. Refer to manufacturer's instructions for additional details. There are other transfer products available that can be used with wood. Choose the one that is easiest for you.

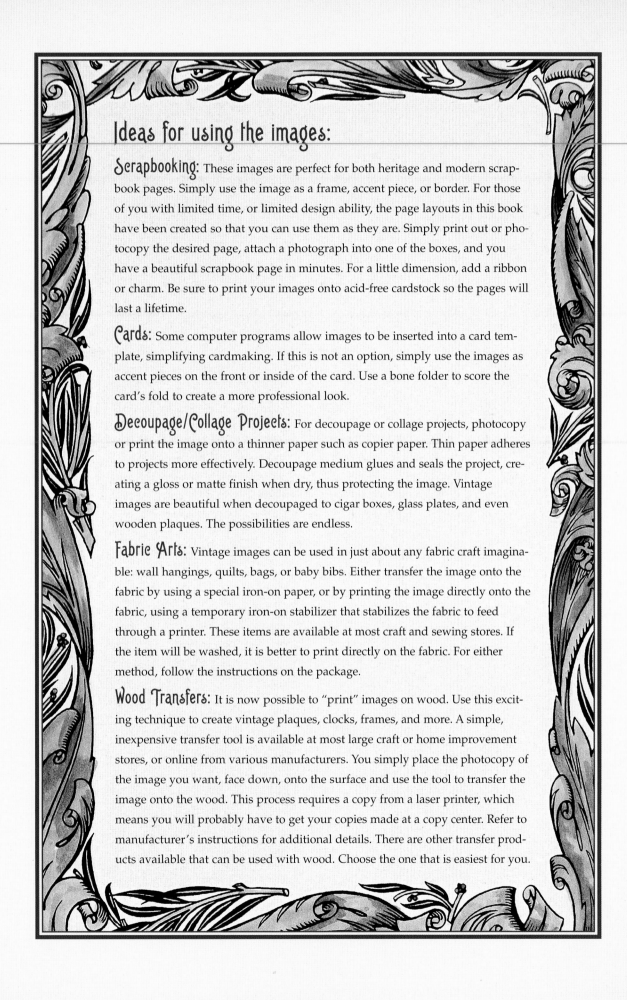

Gallery of ideas

These frame and border designs can be used in a variety of projects: both traditional and nontraditional scrapbook pages as well as cards, decoupage projects, framed pieces, and fabric transfers, just to name a few. The images can be used as presented in their original layouts or you can photocopy and clip out the individual images, portions of images, or multiples of images. The following pages contain a collection of ideas to inspire you to use your imagination and create one-of-a-kind projects.

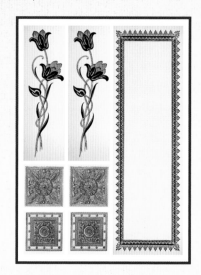

A Mother's Scrapbook Page

Steven

Elizabeth

Tom & Kurt

A Mothers Love

Before you were conceived I wanted you Before you were born I loved you Before you were here an hour I would die for you This is the miracle of life.

Maureen Hawkins

This scrapbook page was created using the original layout design. A photograph was used in place of the two floral borders. Two photographs and two nameplates were substituted for the four small square borders. In this instance, we have completed the page design and layout work for you.

This initial scrapbook page was photocopied and used as is. Vintage photographs were added to the small calendar pages in each of the boxes. This can be accomplished by using computer-generated graphics, or you can simply crop three photographs to fit and attach them to the page.

Sweet Baby Scrapebook Page

The border pieces were used to convey important information about the photographs. This can also be accomplished by the use of computer-generated graphics or the information can be hand-written.

Notebooks are a very much appreciated small gift. This notebook was made by cutting two pieces from cardstock to the desired size of the notebook. Several pieces of heavy scrapbook paper were then cut ¼" smaller on both sides and ½" shorter than the cover pieces.

Memories Notebook

Two grommets were inserted into the top of the notebook. Thread was tied through each grommet and around a small round wooden dowel. A ribbon and flowers were then adhered to the dowel.

For the front of the notebook, a frame was photocopied from this book and cut out. The center was removed and a new center was added, on which a computer-generated saying had been printed. These two pieces were then adhered to the front of the notebook. Adornments were added for a finishing touch.

Memory is a way of holding onto the things you love, the things you are, the things you never want to lose.

Family Scrapbook Page

Truly beautiful scrapbook pages are very quickly created by using the frames and borders printed in this book. For this scrapbook page, one of the frames was photocopied and cut out. The center was removed and a vintage photograph was attached. A strip of loosely woven ribbon was attached to a scrapbook page, the frame and photograph were adhered on top, a small tag was created with the word "family" stamped on it. A ribbon was threaded through the eye of the tag, then the tag was attached to the page with a foam dot. Two buttons were added for accent. This page was completed in less than 10 minutes.

Memory Box

This box was made by using one of the frame designs in the book. The center image of the design was cut out and set aside. The frame was then adhered to the top of a painted and antiqued wooden box. Small adornments were adhered to the lid and to the front of the box, along with a vintage closure. Miniature silk flower petals were adhered to the center of the box, forming a decorative border.

On the box bottom, a second frame image was used along with a small heart button. This memory box is a wonderful gift for a teenage girl, a grandmother, or a special friend.

On the inside of the box, the cut-out center of the design was then used as a photograph. The words for the message are "rub-ons" that were applied.

This card was created by cutting a piece from yellow cardstock and a piece from scrapbook paper to the same size and shape—an uneven square. The two pieces of paper were then stitched, wrong sides together, on the sewing machine. Very small rivets were added in each corner of the square, then ribbons were threaded through and knotted to hold them in place.

Flower Thank~You Card

A frame was photocopied from the images in this book, then carefully cut out. It was adhered to the inside of the card with several foam dots to give it dimension. A thank-you tag was then created with computer-generated graphics, cut to fit the center of the frame, and adhered with foam dots. This card should be packaged in a box before sending it through the mail.

Decorative Handkerchief

This beautiful personalized handkerchief was made by using a computer imaging program to add text to the desired image. The images were printed onto iron-on transfer paper in mirror-image mode. The images were then cut out and ironed onto the handkerchief. If you do not have access to imaging software, the name can be written by hand or embroidered onto the handkerchief once the design is in place.

Old Friend Thank~You Card

This card was created by cutting a rectangle from cardstock to the desired size. A piece of scrapbook paper was torn and adhered in the center of the rectangle. A row of stitching was then sewn around the edge of the rectangle, using a sewing machine. Two frame images were photocopied from this book, then cut out. They were adhered to the card front with foam dots for dimension. A third frame with a message was created on the computer, then adhered with a foam dot. Rivets were added to both sides of the card and a ribbon was tied through for a closure. A handwritten message can be added to the inside.

THE BEST MIRROR
IS AN OLD FRIEND
SPANISH PROVERB

ThanK You

BF01-003   BF01-002

BF01-004   BF01-005

BF02-001

BF03-003

BF03-002

BF03-004

BF03-005

BF04-002

BF04-003   BF04-004

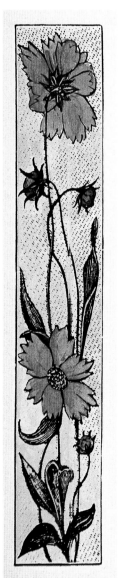

BF05-003   BF05-002

BF05-004   BF05-005

BF06-006

BF06-005

BF06-004

BF06-003

BF06-002

BF06-007

BF06-008

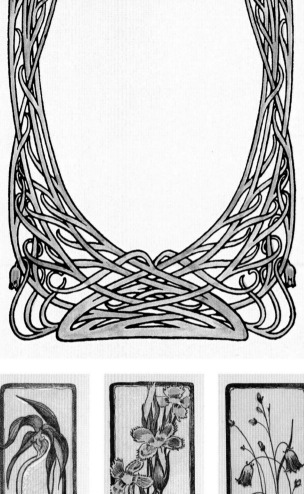

BF07-002

BF07-003　　　　　BF07-011　　BF07-010　　BF07-009

BF07-006　　BF07-005　　BF07-004　　　　　BF07-008

BF07-007

7　BF07-001

BF08-003

BF08-002

BF08-004

BF08-005

BF08-006

BF08-001

8

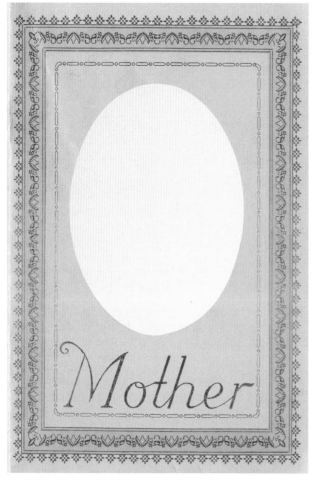

Mother

The Changing Year

The Stork brought a _____
Name _____
Date _____

JANUARY

See,
Winter comes, to rule the varied year,
Sullen and sad, with all his
rising train,
Vapours, and clouds, and storms.

Thomson

FEBRUARY

Up in the morning's no for me,
Up in the morning early;
When a' the hills are cover'd wi' snaw,
I'm sure its winter fairly.

Burns

MARCH

The stormy March is come at last,
With wind, and cloud, and
changing skies,
I hear the rushing of the blast
That through the snowy
valley flies.
Bryant.

APRIL

It was an April
morning,
fresh
and clear,
The Rivulet, delighting in
its strength,
Ran with a young
man's speed.
Wordsworth.

THE STORK AND CUPID ARRANGED A PLOT
TO BRING TO OUR HOUSE A LITTLE TOT.
It's a _____ weighing _____ pounds
And named _____
Mr. and Mrs. _____
Date _____

BF09-003

BF09-002

BF09-004

BF09-006

BF09-005

BF09-001

BF10-003   BF10-002

                    BF10-004   BF10-006

                    BF10-005

Among
the changing
months,
May stands
confest
The sweetest,
and in fairest
colours dressed.

Thomson.

JUNE

And after her came
jolly June, array'd
All in greene leaves,
as he a player were.

Spenser.

JULY

Bright Summer
comes along
the sky
And paints the
glowing
year,
Where'er we turn the raptured eye
Her splendid
tints appear.

Leigh Hunt.

AUGUST

Now ere sweet
Summer
bids its
long
adieu,
And winds blow keen where
late the blossom grew,
The bustling day and jovial
night must come.
Bloomfield.

SEPTEMBER

The
gentle Wind
a sweet
and passionate
wooer,
Kisses the blushing leaf,
and stirs up life
Within the solemn woods
Longfellow.

OCTOBER

Gone the
Summer's pomp
and show,
and

Autumn, in his
leafless bower
Is waiting for
the Winter's snow.
Whittier.

BF11-005   BF11-004   BF11-003   BF11-002

BF11-007

BF11-006

BF11-001

BF12-005   BF12-004   BF12-003   BF12-002

BF12-006

BF12-007

Alas! how changed from the fair scene
When birds sang out their
merry lay,
And winds
were soft,
and woods
were green.

NOVEMBER

Longfellow

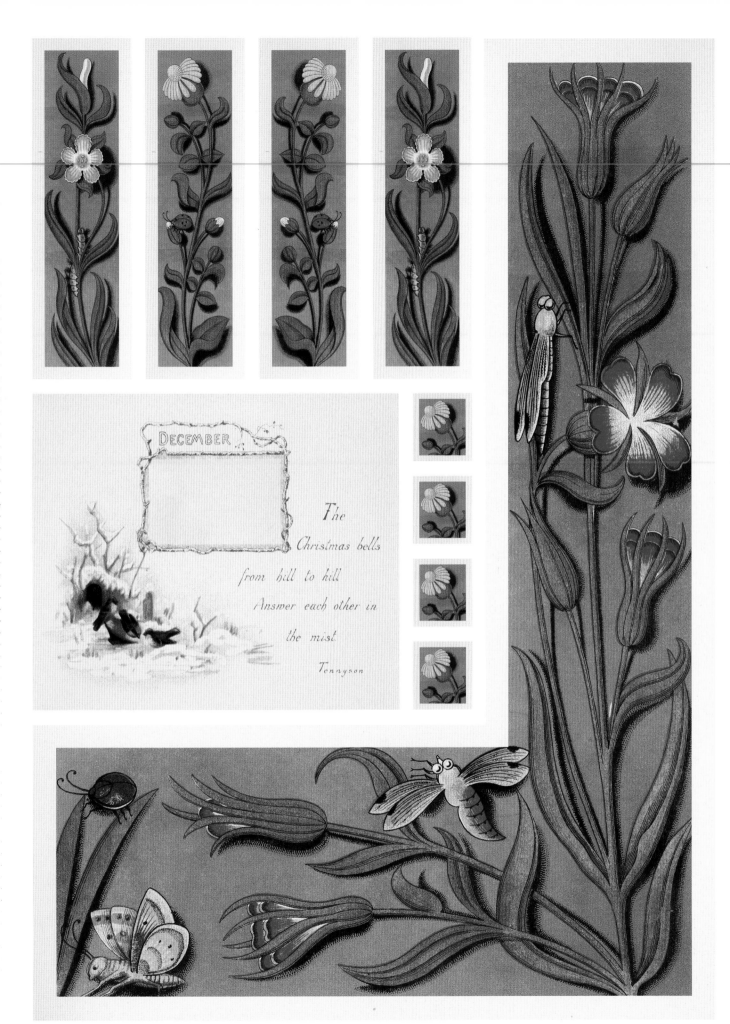

DECEMBER

The

Christmas bells

from hill to hill

Answer each other in

the mist.

Tennyson

BF13-005

BF13-004   BF13-003   BF13-002

BF13-007

BF13-006

BF13-001

BF14-001

BF15-003

BF15-002

BF15-005

BF15-004

15 — BF15-001

BF16-003

BF16-004   BF16-002

BF16-005

BF16-006   BF16-007   BF16-008

BF17-003

BF17-002

BF17-004

BF17-008

BF17-007

BF17-005

BF17-006

BF18-001

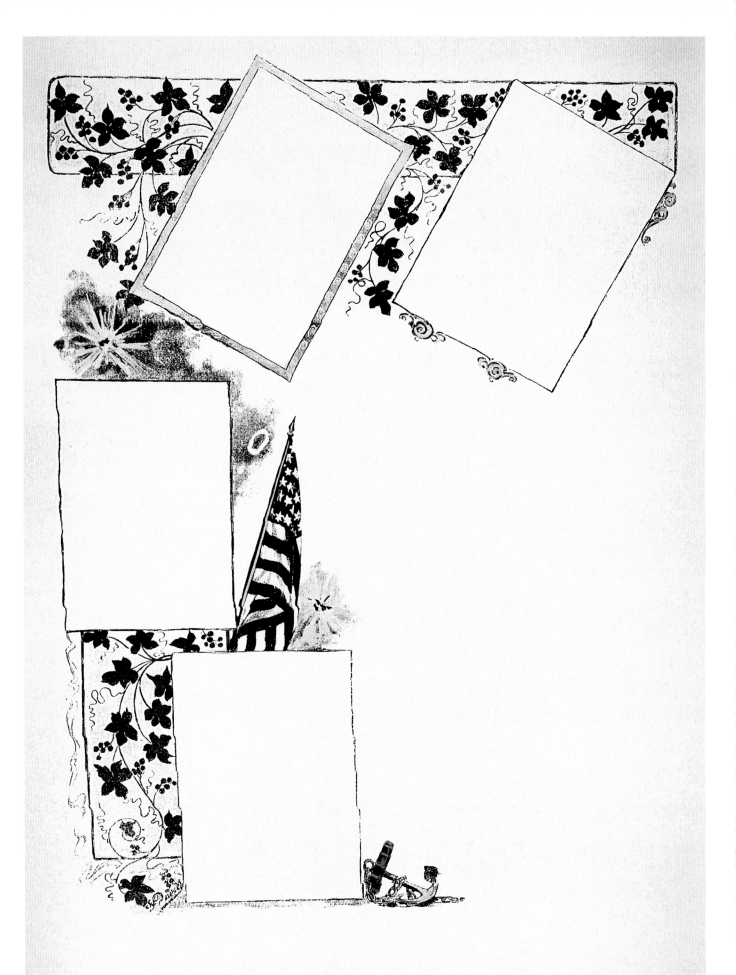

BF19-001

BF20-001

BF21-001

BF22-001

BF23-003   BF23-002

                BF23-004

BF23-005   BF23-006

BF23-001

BF24-003   BF24-002

BF24-004   BF24-007

BF24-005   BF24-006

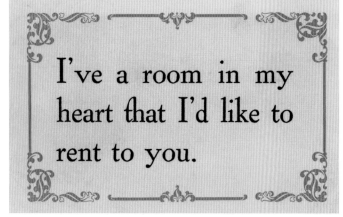

I've a room in my
heart that I'd like to
rent to you.

A TOKEN OF LOVE

BF25-003

BF25-002

BF25-007

BF25-004

BF25-005

BF25-006

BF25-001

BF26-001

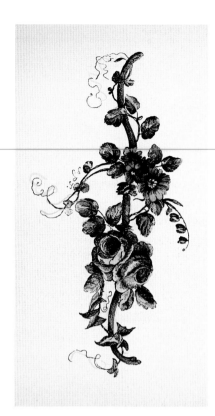

BF27-004   BF27-003   BF27-002

BF27-005   BF27-007

BF27-006

— BF27-001

BF28-001

BF29-002

BF29-004

BF29-003

BF29-001

BF30-001

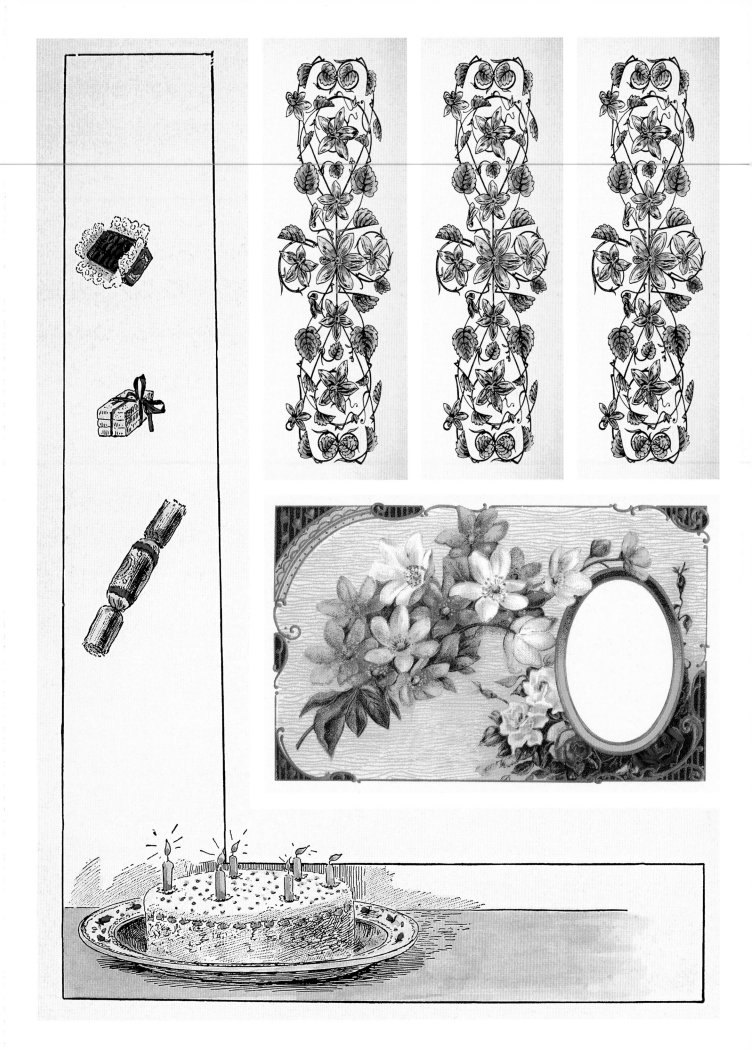

BF31-003

BF31-002

BF31-004

BF32-003

BF32-002

BF32-004

BF32-008

BF32-007

BF32-005

BF32-006

BF32-001

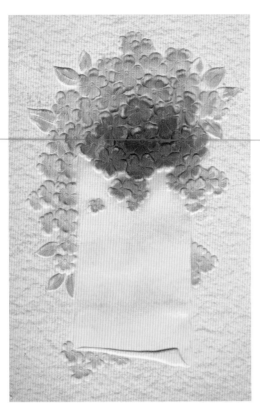

BF33-004

BF33-003

BF33-002

BF33-005

BF33-009

BF33-006

BF33-007

BF33-008

BF33-001

BF34-001

BF35-002

BF35-003   BF35-004

BF35-001

BF36-001

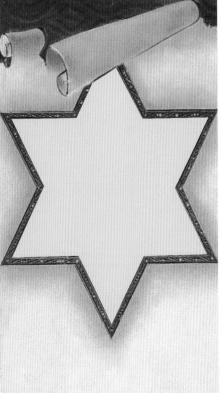

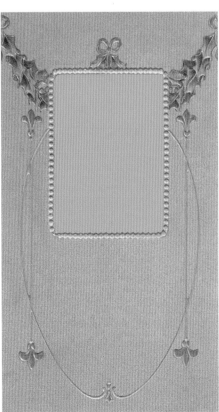

BF37-002

BF37-003   BF37-004   BF37-005

BF37-001

BF38-001

BF39-002

BF39-003

BF39-004

BF40-003

BF40-002

BF41-002

BF41-003

BF41-004

BF41-001

BF42-003

BF42-002

BF42-004

BF42-005

BF42-001

BF43-003

BF43-002

BF43-005

BF43-004

43 — BF43-001

BF44-003

BF44-002

BF44-004

BF44-005

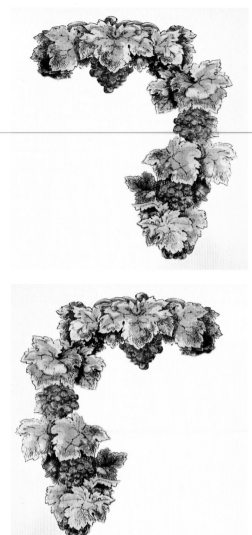

BF45-003

BF45-002

BF45-004

BF45-005

BF45-006

BF45-001

BF46-001

BF47-001

BF48-003   BF48-002

BF48-004

BF49-002

BF49-003   BF49-006

BF49-004   BF49-005

BF49-001

BF50-001

BF51-004   BF51-003   BF51-002

BF51-005   BF51-006

51 — BF51-001

BF52-002

BF52-003   BF52-004

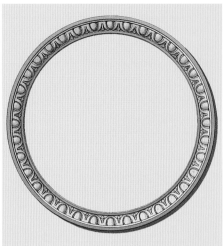
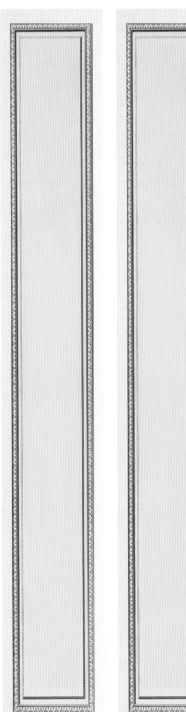

BF53-003   BF53-002

BF54-001

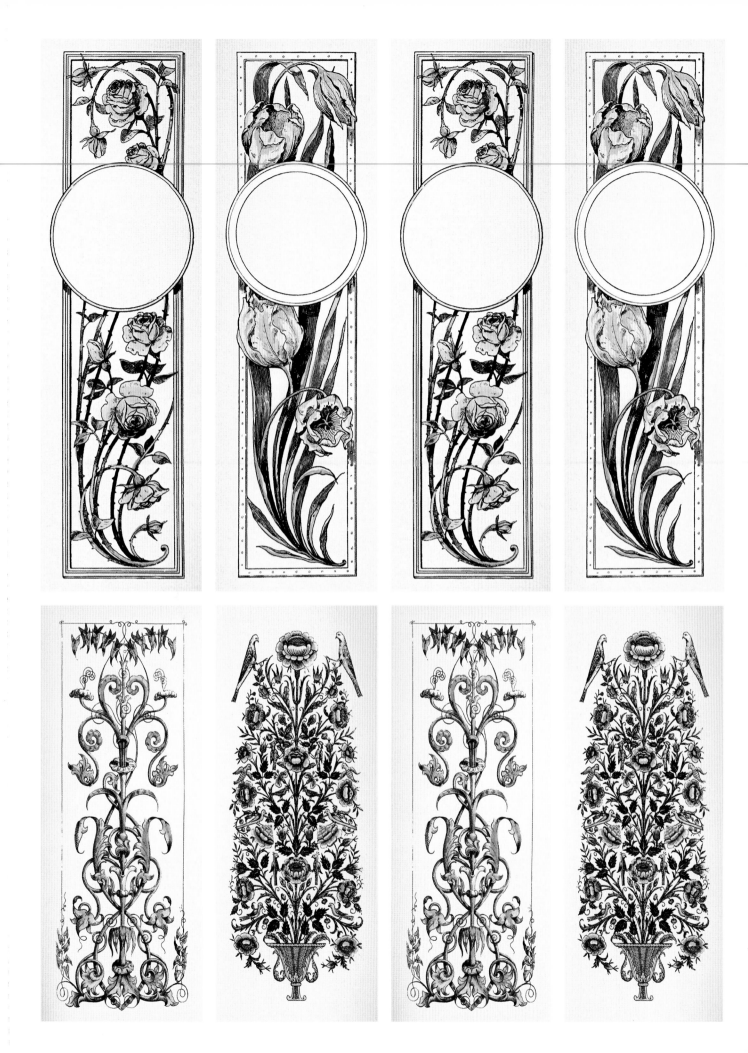

BF55-003   BF55-002

BF55-004   BF55-005

BF56-003

BF56-002

BF56-004

BF56-005

BF57-003   BF57-002

BF57-004

BF57-005   BF57-006

BF57-001